THE SPIRIT OF
CONWY: 1
THE 20TH CENTURY IN PHOTOGRAPHS

E. M. Pattinson O.B.E.

DEDICATION

The Honey Fair

LANDMARK COLLECTOR'S LIBRARY

THE SPIRIT OF
CONWY: 1
THE 20TH CENTURY IN PHOTOGRAPHS

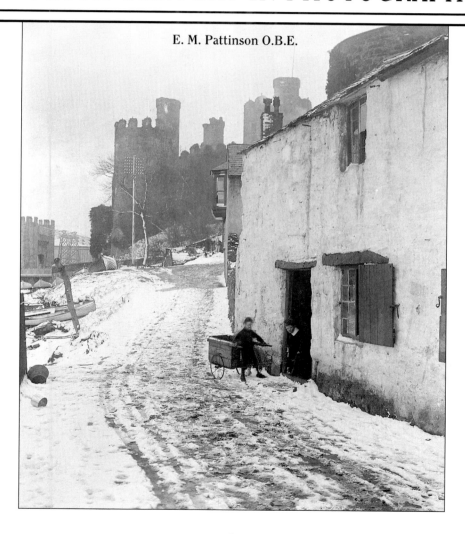

E. M. Pattinson O.B.E.

Landmark Publishing

Published by

Landmark Publishing Ltd
Ashbourne Hall, Cokayne Ave, Ashbourne, Derbyshire DE6 1EJ England
Tel: (01335) 347349 Fax: (01335) 347303
e-mail: landmark@clara.net
web site: www.landmarkpublishing.co.uk

ISBN 1 901522-81-4

Print: Bookcraft, Midsomer Norton
Design: Mark Titterton
Cover: James Allsopp

Front cover: Conwy Castle with the toll arch and old fire station.
Back cover top: The steam packet to Trefriw showing the collapse of one of the castle towers;
Middle: Celebrating the centenary of the tubular bridge; **Bottom:** Aberconwy House, Castle Street.
Title page: The R'odyn.

CONTENTS

The Parish Church of St Mary & All Saints ... 9

The Castle and its Environs ... 17

The Bridges ... 35

Lancaster Square & Bangor Road Arch ... 50

High Street ... 62

Castle Street & Berry Street ... 70

Rosehill Street & Church Street ... 85

Uppergate Street & Rosemary Lane ... 87

The R'odyn ... 92

Other Scenes ... 97

Conwy Postcards ... 101

A Day With Royalty ... 106

Other Visitors ... 113

Proclamations & Coronation Celebrations ... 116

Telford 150 ... 122

Civic Events ... 126

The opening of Bodlondeb ... 126

Office of Mayor/Constable of the Castle ... 129

Gatherings at the Castle ... 147

Funerals & Remembrance ... 148

Teaching our Children ... 160

Social & Other Events ... 169

Visitors ... 183

INTRODUCTION

During the 19th century, the crossings of the river brought enormous changes to the town of Conwy. During the 20th century, the building of the first "immersed tube tunnel" in Great Britain has also made an impact on Conwy, taking out the heavy lorries which once thundered through our ancient town where we are surrounded by legacies of many centuries. Conwy is a very important part of the rich tapestry that forms our European heritage and it and its environs must be protected; we owe it to the future, and to those who come after us.

The heart of a town is not in its buildings, but in its people, amd in the following pages, whilst certain buildings will bring back memories, there are many photographs of special occasions which people celebrated. Over the centuries, Conwy has attracted many visitors, including all six monarchs of the 20th century (from Queen Victoria to our present Queen) also the three Princes of Wales, many politicians, artists, eminent engineers and millions of people who love our town.

I do hope that you will enjoy Book 1, which is mainly confined to the walled town, and which will extend to at least one more book after this. Book 2 will contain the harbour, pageants, Morfa, Gyffin, Deganwy, Llandudno Junction etc.

With the change in name – Conway to Conwy, the latter spelling has been adopted throughout, including references to the name prior to the change for reasons of consistency.

Betty Pattinson, Conwy, September 2002

ACKNOWLEDGEMENTS

I wish to place on record my appreciation to the photographers who took the photographs in this book. Many are dead – their work lives after them. In particular I would like to mention my old friend W W Harris who enjoyed recording history and to whom Conwy owes a debt. I have endeavoured to ask permission from those I know, as for the latter ones, it has not always been possible to attribute them, and I apologise if I've used any without permission.

I wish to thank my husband for his help in collecting photographs and postcards over the years and his friends who have drawn his attention to relevant material for sale. My thanks also to my family, friends, colleagues and staff of Conwy Town Council for their encouragement.

Thanks also to Mrs G Simpson, Mrs B Foulkes, Mr W Evans, Mr G Davis, Mr D Roberts, Mr T Taylor, Mr D Roberts, North Wales Weekly News, and the National Library of Wales.

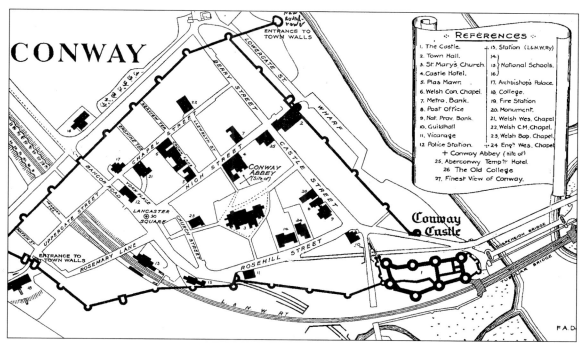

Town plan of Conwy, 1901 drawn by F A de la Motte, Borough Surveyor, 19th July, 1901

Prince Llewelyn monument, Conwy. In Lancaster Square there is a statue of Llewelyn at Iorweth, Founder of Conwy Abbey, A.D. 1184 which surmounts a handsome fountain bearing the following subscription: "The Corporation of Conway engrave this plate to record their gratitude for this fountain, presented to the town by Albert Wood, D L , J.P. of Bodlondeb (a former mayor of the Borough) – Charles J Wallace, mayor, 1898". It is said that Llewelyn the Great is looking towards the Abbey of Aberconwy which he founded. The foundations were marked out in 1172 A.D. and it is generally accepted that it was completed in 1186 A.D. The abbey was incorporated into the Cistercian Order the following year, and is included in the list of Cistercian abbeys in one of the Cottonian MSS at the British Museum.

The abbey of Aberconwy was virtually the Westminster Abbey of Wales. It was at this abbey that Llewelyn the Great (Llewelyn Fawr) was buried in a monk's cowl to ward off the evil eye, and it became a mausoleum for native princes; about five were buried there. Llewelyn Fawr's body was buried in 1240 A.D. and later was moved to Maenan, when Edward I moved the Abbey to there, so that he could have his garrison church at Conwy. He treated the monks very fairly. Today Prince Llewelyn's empty coffin can be seen at Llanrwst church. Legend says that it was found in a field being used as a trough. The body could have been taken back to Conwy

The Parish Church of St Mary & All Saints

The church was formerly the Abbey of Aberconwy – it was a depository for National Records of Wales and public acts and was also renowned for its library. In 1245 an English army, stationed at Deganwy under Henry III, plundered the abbey. A letter written on 24th September of that year, by a nobleman in the King's army, refers to operations on the western bank of the Conway, and declares that "amongst other profane proceedings they irreverently pillaged a Convent of the Cistercians called Aberconwy, of all its properties, and even of the chalices and books, and burnt the buildings belonging to it".

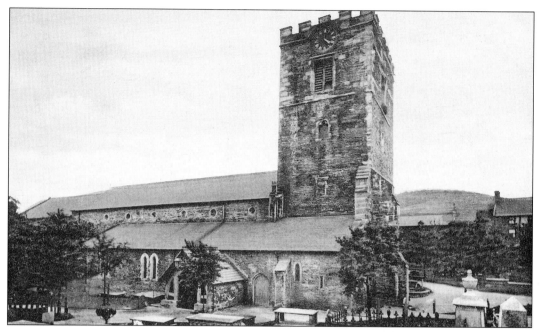

This interior shows the font, also the words over the altar which were covered over many years ago. The font is 15th century with a moulded octagonal base. The pedestal and bowl panels are moulded and decorated with tracery. It replaces an earlier font and is considered to be unique. Amongst the thousands who have been christened at the font were two great Welshmen: 27th March, 1582 – John Williams, Archbishop of York and John Gibson, the famous sculptor, in 1790

Words over altar (covered during alterations):
"CYSEGR PRESWYLFEYDD Y GORUCHAF" — "The Holy dwelling place of the Almighty"

This photographs shows the font, pews and screen. Many of the previous pews were removed in 1872 during extensive alterations by Sir Gilbert Scott. Prominent families used to have brass plates with their names on their pews also some pews had doors which were locked and there used to be pew rents

The Screen is considered to be the finest in North Wales it must have been an imposing structure with its rood, parapet, tracery and running patterns on the front and back beams on the left floor levels. It is said to be late 15th century. The carvings along the top beam showed various Tudor devices such as a rose, dragon, falcon and running greyhound; the three feathers are for Arthur, Prince of Wales, and the gull grasping a foot is for Sir Richard Pole who was Constable of Conwy Castle in 1488

The Memorial chapel was dedicated by the Bishop of Bangor to 56 men of the parish who died in the First World War. In the Memorial chapel, there is a book in a glass case honouring those who gave their lives in the Second World War, including former choir boys. "We will remember them"

Old lace dated 15th century, presented by the FitzHammond family to Conwy Church, 1721

Outside St Mary's Church, with Mr R Williams and Mr E Roberts to the left of the dog

The Grave immortalized by Wordsworth's Poem

"We are Seven"

I met a little cottage girl;
  She was eight years old, she said;
Her hair was thick with many a curl
  That clustered round her head.

"Sisters and brothers, little maid,
  How many may you be?"
"How many? seven in all," she
  said,
  And wondering, looked at me.

"And where are they? I pray you
  tell,"
  She answered, "Seven are we;
And two of us at Conway dwell,
  And two are gone to sea.

Two of us in the church-yard lie,
  My sister and my brother;
And, in the church-yard cottage, I
  Dwell near them with my mother."

"You say that two at Conway dwell,
  And two are gone to sea,
Yet ye are seven! I pray you tell,
  Sweet maid, how this may be."

"Their graves are green, and may be
  The little maid replied,   [seen;"
"Twelve steps or more from my
  mother's door
  And they are side by side.

My stockings there I sometimes
  knit,
  My kerchief there I hem;
And there upon the ground I sit,
  And sing a song to them.

And often after sunset, Sir,
  When it is light and fair,
I take my little porringer,
  And eat my supper there."

The old sun dial inscribed "Robert Wynne jun., Esq., Alderman Hugh Williams & John Nuttal, Bailiffs 1761 – Meredith Hughes fecit, Disce bene vivere et mori"

Coming out of Conwy church – Civic Sunday. From left: Bennett Valentine Hughes J.P., A L Ralphes (Town Clerk), Canon Gwynfryn Richards. Note the woman's face carved on the wall, the headress gives away the date of this beautiful arch: c. 14th century

The marble bust to John Gibson the famous sculptor, baptised in Conwy church in 1790. It was said that he began his career by sketching the many inn signs in Conwy. The then Prince of Wales (afterwards Edward VII) was a contributor to the memorial. John Gibson was buried in Rome and if you study the memorial, one side seems to have oak leaves on it and the other side laurel leaves

The old porch

The Castle and its Environs

World Heritage Status

On 1st January, 1987, the four castles at Caernarfon, Conwy, Harlech and Beaumaris, along with the Town Walls at Caernarfon and Conwy, were officially designated as World Heritage Sites.
In recognition of this prestigious listing, Cadw: Welsh Historic Monuments commissioned four individual plaques for the castles which were unveiled on 5th May, 1988.

The approach to Conwy from the east, with the view of the castle above the river, must be one of the most impressive in the Kingdom.

This early postcard shows Conwy Castle from the south – considered to be one of the finest views of an ancient monument in Great Britain. The castle and walls were built by Edward I

Conwy Castle and the bridges in 1909, a scene familiar all over the world

Two views (above and opposite top page) showing Conwy Castle before the castle wall was taken down to enlarge Castle Square for traffic. It also shows the steps which led from the old entrance into the castle. The bridge is beyond the archway

A Welsh Parish Tea in aid of Conwy Church, held in the Vicarage gardens c. 1960

Now known as Chapel Tower. The plaque shown is now kept in the Guildhall

This view shows the toll arch, old fire station and a break in the castle wall

1st May 1934. A new entrance to the Conwy Suspension Bridge has now been made to expedite the passage of traffic. The old fire station and part of the ancient castle walls have been demolished to carry out this scheme. Note the left side of the view now has railings

The site of the old fire station, showing the old ladder and the break in the castle wall. The view is towards the town

Conwy Castle, "The hole in the wall" 20th May 1934. The view is towards the suspension bridge

The town walls on the south side of the castle in 1913

The town walls on the south side showing the broken tower (later repaired by the Railway Company). The regular Steam Packet "St George" is shown in Gyffin Stream. It ran from Conwy to Trefriw. The advert on the paddlewheel reassures readers that the excursion included the trip back!

The town walls, near the Mill Gate, showing the finest examples of "medieval latrines" in the country

Above left: The seal of the corporation. E DE CONEWWY SY PROVESTRI – Edward Gave Conway The Seal For The Provost. (Now used by Conway Town Council). *Above right:* The logo of the Walled Towns Friendship Circle. The local link consists of: Caernarfon, Chester, Conwy & Denbigh and Beaumaris. The last named town joined this link in 2001. There are 150 walled towns belonging to the main link, as far away as China.

South side Conwy Castle, showing the timber yard and Steam Packet

Conwy Castle and Tubular Bridge in 1908

Lowergate Street in 1911 showing houses; the smallest house; pub (Royal Oak); and arch in the Wing Gate Wall (Porth yr Aden). Through the arch was a pub called the Joiners' Arms

Above left: Uppergate Street Arch (Porth Ucha) from Uppergate Street, showing the college through the arch. View taken in 1910. *Above right:* Another view from Sychnant Pass Road, showing more detail of the wall

Above left: Uppergate Street Arch from the Sychnant Pass Road in 1932. Note the plus fours (trousers). There were formerly thatched cottages where the houses can be seen through the arch. *Above right:* Lowergate Arch (Porth Isa)

Above left: Another view of the Lowergate Arch. Note the shops on the left. *Above right:* Quay Arch, looking towards Lowergate Street. This arch is usually used as the entrance to the Marine Walk. On old plans Lowergate Street was known as The Strand. *Below left:* The toll gate and fire station. *Below right:* The toll gate arch

The Mill Gate Arch (Porth y Felin). Note the Old Vicarage on the left. There was a Horse Mill Farm in this area, possibly before the vicarage was built.

Porth y Sarn, gateway to Gyffin

Above left: Porth y Sarn (Gateway to the Causeway). The area where the Bowling Green is situated is called Pen Sarn. *Above right:* Bangor Road Arch where there was a Gent's Urinal on the right. *Below left:* Bangor Road Arch showing houses on the right. These were demolished in a scheme to clear the Conwy walls. Gwydr House; the ambulance station; the fire station; the mortuary; and small businesses were removed to open up a superb vista of the walls from the bottom of Town Ditch Road to the top of Mount Pleasant

Above: Berry Street Arch which was built in the 20th century by A Wood to allow carriages to go to Bodlondeb. On the right and also on the left at different dates, there used to be a pound for stray animals. Wandering preachers were allowed to preach in this area; it was called 'Bedlam Barracks'. There was also a tavern near here called 'Soldiers Rest'.

Mill Gate, with the railway goods yard and medieval latrines high on the castle wall

Building the stone road bridge at Rosemary Lane, for Conwy Station. One of the stone lions is still to be seen on the Bangor side of Rosemary Lane Road; the other disappeared during reconstruction of the road

Conwy Railway Station, designed by Francis Thompson. On one occasion there was a major fire here. A former station master in the 19th century was well known because he grew lilies at the station

Steam train leaving Conwy Tubular Bridge

"The Rocket" in 1948. This replica was part of the celebrations marking the building of the Tubular Bridge in 1848 by Robert Stephenson

Conwy Station – railway staff in 1909

After a long fight to re-instate a halt at Conwy (after the station had been demolished under Dr Beeching's axe), one was finally opened on the 27th June 1987

A steam train on Gyffin Railway Arch, engine no. 2522

This engraving shows the building of the tubular bridge, the twin parts being floated into position before being lifted into place in 1848. The engineer was Robert Stephenson, son of George Stephenson

Conwy Castle and the Tubular Bridge. In recent years the bridge was painted blue by the Railway Authorities. However, common sense prevailed and they were repainted stone colour, as shown on original prints

Thomas Telford's graceful Suspension Bridge, built in 1826. Now in the hands of the National Trust, it has been described as the historical gateway to Conwy. In building his bridge, the Water Gate to the castle was destroyed, although one can still see the steps

Opening the pedestrian bridge adjoining Thomas Telford's Bridge. This shows the mayor and members of Conwy Borough Council in 1904. This bridge has now been demolished. This pedestrain bridge was built in 1894 by T B Farrington C.E. to convey water from Cowlyd Lake to Conwy, Deganwy and Colwyn Bay. It was removed following the erection of the new road bridge

The three bridges: Telford's bridge, the Water Bridge and R Stephenson's railway bridge in 1922. How wonderful it was when we won the enquiry not to have a monstrosity of a further bridge built near the castle. This would have dwarfed the south side of Conwy Castle & Walls and was the preferred scheme in the 1970s

Guarding Conwy Bridge in 1916 during the First World War by the Conwy Platoon (1st C.V.R Bridge Guard). An elderley artist told me years ago that when he was a young man, at the time of the Great War, he sketched Conwy Bridge & Castle and was promptly arrested!

Painting Conwy Suspension Bridge before the Second World War. This was usually undertaken by Conwy fishermen between seasons. Note the Water Bridge on the left

The famous view of the Castle and its three Bridges

"The Cob" – the bridge embankment – before it was laid out as a promenade

The Island (Yr Ynys). This was set out as a park, with seats and trees in 1888-9 (during the mayoralty of Coun. Thomas Abram). The Island was illuminated for the Coronation of Edward VII in 1902, when the Castle was lit up and fireworks were discharged from a barge on the river creating a spectacular display. It was destroyed when the new road bridge was built in 1958

Building the 1958 Road Bridge

A dramatic view of the bridge before the joining of the two halves, high above the river. The position looks rather precarious for the men

The official opening 13th December, 1958

The first traffic streams over to the east bank of the river

The Embankment locally known as "the Cob". This was known as "Conwy's Promenade"

Thomas Telford, the greatest Civil Engineer of the late 18th and early 19th century designed the first bridge to span the river at Conwy. It became one of the most photographed bridge of all times. Its castellated towers echoing the medieval towers above it. It was in danger of being demolished about forty years ago, but was saved by the strength of feeling of the local people, led by the late Miss Agnes Hughes, a former mayor. She formed a committee called "Save Conway Bridge Appeal", meeting in another former mayor's house, in Parry Watch. We received support from throughout the Borough and even from abroad. The result was that the National Trust took the graceful bridge into its care. The National Trust has restored the bridge and the toll house has been furnished as it would have been more than a century ago.

The illustration shows a leaflet which records a poll of electors on the future of the bridge

The former railway crossing gates, which caused so many queues. The Maelgwyn Hotel is to be seen on the right

OFFICIAL OPENING

of the

CONWY TUNNEL

by

HER MAJESTY THE QUEEN

Friday 25 October 1991

The programme for the official opening of the first immersed tube tunnel in Great Britain by H.M. The Queen, Friday 25th October, 1991

A55 North Wales Coast Road
Conwy Crossing

Welsh Office

G Mercer, CEng FICE FIHT MIStructE,
Director of Highways, Transport & Highways Group

Work started on the Conwy Crossing in November 1986. Construction is being undertaken by the Costain Tarmac Joint Venture. The work is being supervised for the Welsh Office by Travers Morgan & Partners, Consulting Engineers, who in association with Christiani & Nielsen A/S, prepared the designs apart from the rail underbridge at Llandudno Junction, supervision of which is undertaken by the Chief Civil Engineer, British Rail (London Midland Region). The Contract value is £102m and the work is due to be completed in four and a quarter years.

The crossing is part of the works to be undertaken to improve the A55 North Wales Coast Road from Chester to Bangor to dual carriageway standards. The road is carried under the Conwy Estuary in a tunnel which was selected following a lengthy public inquiry and having regard to the preservation of the setting of Conwy Castle as one of Britain's most imposing national monuments.

Consulting Engineers   Travers Morgan & Partners

in association with   Christiani & Nielsen A/S

Above and overpage: Details of the new Conwy Crossing. The consulting engineers were Travers Morgan & Partners in association with Christiani & Neilson A/S. The contractors were Costain and Tarmac. I don't think the consulting engineers received enough recognition for the wonderful landscaping they did to protect the view from the castle

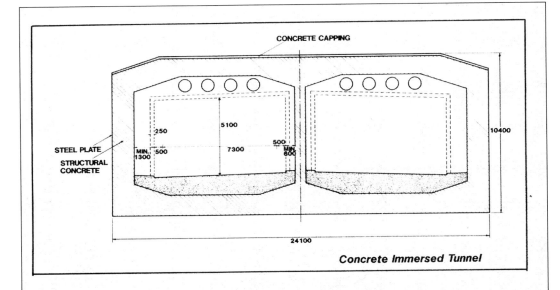

CONCRETE CAPPING

STEEL PLATE

STRUCTURAL
CONCRETE

250

5100

MIN.
1300

500

7300

500

MIN.
600

10400

24100

Concrete Immersed Tunnel

The tunnel forms part of the A55 North Wales Coast Road between Glan Conwy and Conwy Morfa; a total length of about 6Km. From a junction at Glan Conwy the route connects with a link road to Llandudno Junction before passing under the causeway which carries the Chester to Holyhead railway and the existing A55. West of the estuary the route passes along the south edge of the Conwy Golf Links to another junction at Conwy Morfa, and continues to join the Penmaenbach/Dwygyfylchi section of A55 currently under construction, west of Sam Parry's Bridge.

Advance contracts were started in late 1985 to reposition some of the moorings in the estuary and also to construct an earthworks bund south of the causeway around the edge of the reclamations thus enabling early mobilisation of dredging activities.

Further information about the Conwy Crossing can be obtained from the Chief Resident Engineer, Mr John Bales, to whom any complaint arising during the construction of the Works should be directed in the first instance. The address to contact is:

Chief Resident Engineer
Penmaen Road
Conwy
Gwynedd LL32 8HB
(Telephone 0492 592159)

St. Michael's Church, Grotto and Calvary. Note the photograph below is the same one, with the plaques on the town wall added in the darkroom!

The re-enactment of the Relief of Mafeking in the present vicarage car park

The Timber Yard of D H Lewis to the south of Conwy Castle. There used to be a mill on this site. The yard manager, W M Evans may be seen in the centre (his arm was damaged by a circular saw). He was the grandfather of Will Owen (Will Bach) of Llandudno Junction

The former College, Uppergate Street. Sometimes called Fawcett College. Mr Fawcett was a teacher. There was a connection with Manchester House, Lancaster Square and the Fawcett family who lived there. The biggest improvement this century was the removal of Ysgol Cadnant (Cadnant School) from this site to expose the walls of Conwy

An early view from the castle, showing Conwy Church. There is no school or St John's Methodist Church, houses etc. The old vicarage however, may be seen along with a little farm called "Bryn y Hall"? There used to be a cocoa house near here

Some of the International Town Criers who cried in Lancaster Square, during an International Walled Towns visit to Conwy. With them is Conwy Mayor, J M Jones

From the left The Plough Inn, Plough Bach and the Georgian building, Plas Ucha. Note that the Baptist Church has not been built. The public bakehouse was in this area and a water pump. Later in World War II an air raid shelter was built and it is still there today

The Coronation 1911. The Plough Inn (on the left); J Thomas (grocer & baker); Station Street, Erskine Refreshment Rooms on right and the horsedrawn coach

Coronation Day 22nd June 1911. Note the piano in the Square

Above: Two postcards of Lancaster Square. This is a postcard written in 1920. Note the smaller corner shop and the Red Lion House on the right. Was the fountain ever moved? It seems nearer the Police Station than it is today

The police station; Tabernacle Chapel; Boot Inn and the corner shop before bay windows were added

Lancaster Square showing London House; Manchester House (established 1874); the Chemist; and the Fish shop

This view shows the original entrance to the police station on Bangor Road; children playing at the fountain and the Plough seat. Note alterations to the corner shop

On the left is Maddick's Temperance Hotel & Café; London House and Star Supply Stores; Manchester House, a double decker coach and men sitting on the Plough seat

Lancaster Square in 1925; the Corner Shop is now Dunphy's Corner, with the old Ship Inn on the right

This photograph shows the deterioration in this once fine Georgian building and Parr's the newsagents on the right, formerly a butcher's shop. It also shows the Baptist Chapel

The Plas Coch Temperance House offered teas, coffee and refreshments. The advert outside also mentions "well aired beds". Behind Plas Coch lies the old cockpit. Known as the Round Room, it was used during the 20th century for many community purposes

The Vicarage Car Park, in former times, with a tennis court adjacent to the town wall, the old vicarage is behind the trees. When demolishing this building crushed cockle and mussel shells were found in the foundations and more have been found at other places in the town. Its kitchen had grave slabs in the cold store for storage!

Lancaster Square with yet another procession

Lancaster Square with a church parade of Royal Engineers stationed at the Morfa Camp

Silver Motor Buses in Lancaster Square

Right: The Post Office in Bangor Road with postmen posing outside. This postcard is dated 1909.

Below: Peter Thomas MP with S Hughes in Lancaster Square on 16 October 1964 being congratulated after his re-election to Parliament

Opposite page: The building on the corner of Lancaster Square and Rosemary Lane, before being occupied by the Midland Bank, now H.S.B.C. Tudor Williams, leather dealer etc., occupied these premises at the time the photograph was taken.

Bangor Road Arch Post Office with the Automobile Palace on the right.
The Grosvenor Café is on the left

The Bangor Road Arch again. The corner shop, for many years, formerly W Rowlands, fruiterer,
grocer & tobacco salesman, later became Waterworths

Another view, this time showing the left side of the street. Fred Jones, (Cook and The Grosvenor Café), and D Owen, butchers are on the left. The Post Office and a shop may be seen on the right

Bangor Road showing a milk cart, with a churn on top. We didn't have milk in bottles in those days. A visiting horsedrawn coach stands on the right

Plas Mawr (it means Big Mansion) in the High Street. Built by R Wynne in 1576, it has had many other uses since. It was let out in tenements and some of the rooms were used as a school. The Royal Cambrian Academy had this building for over a century, including the Victorian Art Gallery which has now been taken down. Many important people have visited the building, including the Duke & Duchess of York in 1899, the Queen of Romania and our own Queen Mother in 1982. When I was presented to her, she asked me about the gardens which surrounded Plas Mawr when it was built. Now superbly restored by Cadw, this award winning building was visited by H.R.H Prince of Wales in 2002. Over the last century many community events have taken place in Plas Mawr

Above left: Plas Mawr with gypsies playing their instruments outside the front entrance.

Above right: A group of boys outside Plas Mawr. A case of "old Wales and young Manchester" according to the rear of the photograph!

Right: The house in Edwardian times with an elegantly dressed lady walking up what was then a quiet street

Plas Mawr interior, as it was before restoration. This room is the Banqueting Hall

Plas Mawr courtyard also prior to restoration

Parry's newsagents (this corner is always called Parry Watch) formerly "The Feathers", headquarters of the 19th century Jackdaw Society. The shop stood on the corner of Bangor Road and Chapel Street

Another view of Parry's newsagents. T Parry was a watchmaker, jeweller and sold fancy goods

Parry's newsagents again! Tea, coffee and refreshments were also sold here

Plas Mawr showing The Calendar Building which has 365 windows and 52 doors. The cobbled stones in front used to have white stones with a date, but the cobbles were moved because of complaints from ladies with high heels and/or prams. This view of Plas Mawr shows the original entrance in Crown Lane which was once called Jongleur's Lane (a jongleur was a juggler or entertainer)

High Street and Plas Mawr. The Old Bull's Head stood behind the present chemist, M & J Williams & Crown Tavern on the left; on the right, the refreshment rooms, lower down the Palace Cinema and F W Woolworth's which were built in the mid 1930's

High Street and Plas Mawr showing Barclays Bank's former premises

Plas Mawr Restaurant in the High Street with children waiting for a meal. Adverts say "Commercial Hotel – well aired beds, hot and cold baths, Soup 2d per bowl"

J Jared William's shop in the High Street. This card was posted on the first night that the new Post Office was opened in Bangor Road 26th May, 1907

Plas Isa Place, off Lower High Street and now demolished

Conwy Fair in Castle Street

Berry Street showing the Swan which was a very strange building with many windows. There is still a Swan Terrace and many recordings of Swan Court

Berry Street Corner with High Street. Old residents called this The Cross (Y Groes). The present Civic Hall was the old market hall and the stocks were here. The loss of this lovely half-timbered building was significant. As a "grouping" with Aberconwy House, it would have enhanced the architectural importance of this part of the town

This scene shows Jones & Son, who were Sanitary Plumbers, Painters & Decorators and also ran a cycle and motor depot

The street scene perhaps at the time of the coronation of George V

Another gathering in Castle Street

Joseph Jones, butchers. This was the old Eagles Inn. It is still called Eagles Buildings on the photograph

A procession in Castle Street; probably the Coronation celebrations in 1911

The top of Castle Street showing the original steps up to the Guildhall, prior to 1925 when the new Council Chamber was built

A crowded scene in Castle Street with a parade in progress

Aberconwy House, described as the "Oldest house in Wales" on this photograph!

Aberconwy House on the right. Note the little girls gathered on the right and little boys on left!

This card is entitled "Conway Arms", referring to Aberconwy House when it was a Temperance Hotel

This sign is huge and would not pass planning laws today! The view is towards Aberconwy House

Castle Street pre 1925. On the left is Joseph Jones, who ran a shoe shop; E B Jones & Co; the Blue Bell sign; the chemists and J P Griffiths on the right

Castle Street. Theo Jones the Victoria Tea Rooms, with the proprietors in the doorway. It was next to Aberconwy House and the shop has been known as Veale's for many years

Aberconwy House was the 'Old Coffee Tavern' when this view was taken

Ralphes, Son & Co Decorators and Ironmongers

The old Town Hall, Cinema and present Civic Hall prior to the fire and rebuilding

The Black Lion in Castle Street once a vicarage (vicar John Brickdall lived here). The date over the doorway is 1589 making it one of the town's oldest properties. A pig market used to be held on a Monday morning near here

The Conwy Fair in Castle Street started and ends this chapter on one of the Town's main streets

The old College on Castle Street. Tradition says that Llewelyn ap Iorweth built a structure there with an abbey. Edward I had a college near to this site. The present house is said to have been built in Elizabethan times. The Stanley (Earls of Derby) crest can still be seen; it portrays an eagle pouncing upon a child

This shows the College as originally built

Berry Street – the late Mrs Elinor Roberts in Welsh costume. It is said to have been called Burial Street, but I have seen it called Stryd y Burum. There were two pubs in this street, the Conwy Castle and Castle View and also a school at 3 Berry Street and two streets where burials took place, Berry Street and Chapel Street

It was at this hotel that the well known authoress, Charlotte Brontë stayed on her wedding tour en-route to Ireland, on the 29th June 1854. Fifty years later, her husband Reverend Arthur Bell Nicholls wrote in reference to the hotel: "We found it very comfortable, and the accommodation very good"

The Erskine Family & Commercial Hotel

A rather old photograph of Rosehill Street with the railway station in the foreground

The Constitutional Club, Church Street, part of the Royal British Legion premises, laid out for a celebration

The College from St Agnes Road

The Old Smithy (between Uppergate Street and Rosemary Lane where the teacher's training unit now is)

Ready for the Carnival: This
was taken in Uppergate Street
near Pool Lane

Uppergate Street showing the
premises of John Jones,
Plumber & Glazier

The Albion Vaults in Uppergate Street. The White Horse was near here too

Uppergate Street showing the Bazaar in 1838 on the right. Further on is Newborough Terrace and the Newbridge Arms mentioned in old guide books

Gypsies, monkey entertaining and
begging in Uppergate Street

The College, later the site of the Central School and Cadnant School

The R'odyn

The R'odyn, a name meaning lime kiln, recalls the days when
limestone and coal were brought to the quay

Above left: The R'odyn again, at low tide *Above right:* The Smallest House, a tourist attraction even
in Edwardian times

The Royal Oak Tavern adjacent to the Smallest House

One fisherman who lived on the R'odyn made grandfather clocks

This house was taken down to make more space for vehicles and pedestrians. Some members of the family who lived here were sailors. The bush by the house was said to be a tea plant brought home by one of them

The Liverpool Arms. There was an old sailor's lodging house adjacent to the Liverpool Arms

The Liverpool Arms again. Note the shop on the left

The Smallest House again with its attendant

The Smallest House and a group of curious boys

Margaret Williams pictured outside the tiny house on the quayside. Her great grandfather, Robert Jones, established it as the smallest in Great Britain. The house, lived in until 1900 when it was condemned for human habitation and made into a showplace, is visited by countless people from all over the world and there is a commentary in 20 languages

The Cenotaph war memorial at the Postern gate, Porth Bach

The former Oakwood Park Hotel. It had an 18-hole golf course, hard and grass tennis courts, ballroom, billiards, etc. Many important people stayed in this hotel, which was on the road to the Sychnant Pass

Mr Albert Wood and Mr and Mrs George Swinford Wood on the verandah at Bodlondeb. They belonged to the firm of Henry Wood & Co. which produced the anchors of Brunel's ship "Great Eastern"

Albert Wood with local children. He was mayor of Conwy 11 times and was Conwy's first honorary freeman

Above left: Albert Wood again with his "personal artillery"! *Above right:* The cenotaph placed by the town wall and unveiled on 19th June, 1921. It was moved to Bodlondeb years later *Below:* Parlwr Mawr (the Archbishop's Palace) seen complete and being dismantled. This building stood at the top of Chapel Street, formerly Union Street. The Old Union Tavern, Carmel and Seion Chapels were all on this street. It was built by John Williams who was born in Conwy. He became Archbishop of York in 1641. He was a Welsh speaking "Jackdaw" the name given to all those born within the walls of Conwy. He was involved in the Civil War and had to change sides to save the civic treasures of the people of Conwy

Park Hall

The Woodlands

Conwy Postcards

A small selection of postcards are included. *Top and middle:* Two comic postcards; both undated. *Bottom:* One for the girls as well as the grandeur. This card is dated 1906

Above left: This card recalls a trip from Conwy to Llandudno in 1904 Above right: Arrived safely in 1907 Below left: A card from the soldiers at Morfa Camp Below right: A comic card of 1911

Castle Street, showing the old college as at the end of the 19th century

A similar card on the corner of Berry Street and High Street. The building on the right later became Bron Castell and is now a fish and chip shop having been rebuilt

Plas Mawr at the end of the 19th century. The stalls sold pickled herrings, onions, shellfish, sweets, etc.

Aberconwy House at the end of the 19th century

This card shows the Coach & Horses Inn on the left (now the Mail Coach) and also the Metropolitan Bank in the High Street. On the right are the King's Head, Castle Hotel and Harp Hotel. There was a medieval hospice on this site called The Spital

Another view in High Street. W Bridge (a bookseller); Plas Mawr; (Bull's Head beyond) and the Crown Inn may be seen

A Day With Royalty

Visit of the then Duke and Duchess of York – 1899 (afterwards King George V and Queen Mary) with the then mayor Dr M G Morgan at Conwy Castle and (overpage) Plas Mawr

Above and below: The Prince of Wales, later Duke of Windsor, in the Castle during his 1923 visit

The Prince of Wales leaving Conwy Castle in 1923, and saluting wounded veterans
of the First World War

H.R.H. Princess
Margaret leaving
Conwy Castle in
1951, with the
mayor B V Hughes
JP, and the Town
Clerk, A L Ralphes

H.R.H. Princess Margaret visits Conwy Castle

H.M. The Queen in Conwy Castle, 1991 on the occasion of the opening of the tunnel

The goat of the Royal Welch Fusiliers (not known as a mascot, but as a member of both the Regular and Territorial Battalions – a goat at the head of the Royal Welch Fusiliers was observed as far back as 1777). In 1884 Queen Victoria presented the first royal goat, a custom which has continued to the present day. The Royal Welch Fusiliers are Freemen of Conwy

E M Pattinson O.B.E. being presented to H.M. The Queen with Wyn Roberts MP looking on

Guests at Llandudno Junction waiting for H.M. The Queen to open the tunnel

David Lloyd George, outside The Smallest House. (l-r): R Williams; D Lloyd George; Mrs Williams; Mrs John Roberts; and Miss Gwladys Roberts

Winston, Rt. Hon D Lloyd George's youngest supporter!

Margaret Thatcher, then leader of the Opposition, visits Conwy. The mayor (E M P) presenting her with a print of Conwy

Proclamations & Coronation Celebrations

The Proclamation of George V, 1910

Conwy Boy Scouts on Coronation Day, 1911 in Rosehill Street

Commemoration Service in 1911 at the Castle

Coronation mugs waiting to be distributed to Conwy school children in 1911

Decorated horse and cart. A "few of the boys" on Coronation Day, 1911

An address at the Conwy Castle on Coronation Day, 1911

Another scene of Coronation Day in 1911

School children in Rosehill Street, Coronation Day, 22nd June, 1911. I think the gentleman on the left of the picture is Mr W Allan, headmaster

A parade to commemorate the coronation of King George V, 1911. 1st Conwy Troop Scouts head the procession with their Drums & Fife Band in Castle Street

Lancaster Square, Coronation 1911. Note the Plough on the right with Plough Bach next door, the Baptist Chapel and the Estate Buildings. Finally a row of men standing on the stone Plough seat

The Coronation parade, 1937 getting ready on the Quay

Another view of The Coronation procession, 1937

The 150th anniversary celebrations of the construction of Thomas Telford's Bridge: (Telford 150) in 1976

We built it (Conwy Church Young Wives), Conwy Jackdaw Society, Royal British Legion

More scenes from Telford 150: *Below:* The Sea Cadets and behind The Army Cadets

Telford 150

A coach carrying Civic Dignitaries

Passing through the crowds here are Conwy Town Council, led by P Williams, the Mace Bearer

The event saw the biggest crowds in Conwy for many years; all the community joined in

Civic Events

The opening of Bodlondeb

The present house at Bodlondeb was erected in 1877 and replaced the original house which was about 80 yards to the north. A house on this site was called "Arcadia". I believe the former house was a Nash house. When I was a child, before it became a public building, I was taken there to see the owners by my aunt and uncle. There were beautiful paintings etc., and goldfish in the pond near to where the cenotaph is today. I remember gravestones in front of the house with dog's names on them; a tree house; rose gardens; and greenhouses with all sorts of fruits growing in them

Rt Hon D Lloyd George and family arriving at Castell Mai in Rosehill Street

Rt Hon D Lloyd George and his wife at Bodlondeb

The Mace Bearer and Firemen on 16th July, 1937 during the opening of
Bodlondeb by D Lloyd George

A civic procession in Rosehill Street with a Guard of Honour of Conwy fireman in brass helmets

A civic procession in 1921

Two further civic processions in 1920 with the boy scouts on the lower photograph

Left: Dr M J Morgan J.P., the mayor in 1899, 1900 and 1908 and honorary freeman of Conwy

Civic procession in Rosehill Street with a Guard of honour for the mayor of Conwy Policemen

Outside The Guildhall. Proclamations, elections etc, were all announced here from the steps

Mayor B V Hughes JP, leaves church on Civic Sunday

Left: The mayor at the cenotaph, Bodlondeb at a civic parade with Rt Hon Wyn Roberts, MP in 1989 prior to the Mayor's Parade seen below

The mayor taking the Civic procession on Plas Mawr steps. The Town band is just coming into view

The Story of the Guildhall

When Edward I built his magnificent Castle and Walls at Conwy, he established an English Colony in the town. There were many ancient Guilds in Conwy in those days and the Craftsmen and Merchants met at the Guild Hall, e.g. Mercers, Tailors, Smiths, Tanners, Weavers, Hammermen, Braziers, Masons, Glovers, Skinners, Silversmiths, Curriers, Cordwainers, Corvisors to name but a few.

The Guildhall has been known by a variety of names, Guildhall, Town Hall, Shire Hall, Common Hall and Common House. Since the 13th century, buildings have stood on this site and adjoining sites, but some of these buildings were removed, the last being the attached cottage and others when Thomas Telford built his beautiful suspension bridge and roads, demolishing the ancient buildings for the construction of Rosehill Street and the present Castle Street, with new buildings being built on some of the empty sites. Old records also show that buildings were burnt down through the ages.

The present Guildhall comprises a large room which is 19th century and the Council Chamber and new entrance which were built in 1925. (We do not know the age of the bell tower). There were a number of extensions built on over the years.

The new refurbishment of both the Old Hall and the Council Chamber has been carried out over the last few years by Conwy Town Council who have employed local craftsmen to do the work. With the help of a Lottery Grant, the paintings and photographs have been restored to their former glory.

1527   "Common House".

1573   The sum of £4.00d was paid to the Alderman by new Burgesses who were Sworn. Putt into the Common Coffer, the revenues of the myles belonging to this town of Conwey for one half year. Town of Conwey for one half year. All the same being bestowed uppon the Makinge of the Burgess Chamber at the Shire Hall ended work the same year.

1592   In the Common House of the Towne of Conwey September 1592.

1613   "The Common House" or Town Hall, of this date was pulled down in 1613 and a market hall was built on its site, with an upper storey for a Common Hall. The second hall has, however, been removed within the last 25 years (circa 1861). It stood in Castle Street near the Castle and opposite Rose Hill Street and abutted on the street. A portion of the front was removed when widening the street early in the present 17th century; and a carved beam bearing the inscription "God save the King James 1613" was also taken away.

1612   "New Guildhall built".
        (Carved beam was taken away)
        "God save King James (1613)"
        A Stuart grate back 1613?
        Nicholas Hookes – Alderman.
        Beneath the hall was the heinous or town prison.

1696   An order signed by Richard Vincent Bulkeley, as Alderman, required that all burgesses should appear at the Guildhall upon the tolling of the "Burgess Bell" if they be within the hearing thereof. Failure meant a fine of 2s.6d.

1752   5th May, 1752. "It is agreed by the Aldermen, Bayliffes and Burgesses at the said General Meeting at the Guildhall in Conway "that whosoever milks or encourages any sheep anywhere but on the other side of the Town Mountain wall shall be fined agreeable to the Aldermen mentioned in the old book which is 3s. 6d. for every such sheep milked, elsewhere unless in close pastures.

1757   Petition of Owen Jonas, late miller "To the Aldermen, Bayliffes and Burgesses now assembled in the Common Room of the Borough of Conway".

1811   Thomas Roberts of the Black Horse, Conway was Headmaster of National School for poorer children in a building on this site.

1837   There is a chest in the Council Room at the Guildhall where the Corporation used to hold their meetings, until they fitted up the Town Hall. It was opened about four years ago (1833), and some papers were found. Many of them had crumbled into dust, everything eligible was preserved; they considered chiefly of accounts, vouchers and the like.

1859   Permission granted for school at 6d. per week provided it did not interfere with the meetings of the corporation and the petty sessions.

1862   April – it was decided to call for tenders for alterations to the Town Hall.

1863   The corporation took possession of the rebuilt Guildhall all 3rd August 1863.

1925   Extensions and improvements of Guildhall ("New Guildhall") £6,500

1926/7 Joint Police Committee – use of Guildhall – £5.00
       Conway Corporation (Cellar under Guildhall – no rent.
       Conway Bridge Commissioners (Hire of Rooms) – £50.00
       Sundry Rents and Lettings – £23.3s. 6d.

1930   Extension of Guildhall – £907. 0s.0d.

1935   Extension of Guildhall – £1160.0s.0d.
       Extension of Guildhall – £856 7.6s.5d.

1936   National Association of Friendly Societies

1937   (Hire of Guildhall) – £1.1s.0d.

Uses of the Guildhall

GUILDS

COUNCIL MEETINGS

POLITICAL MEETINGS

COURTS

COMMISSIONERS (BRIDGE)

COMMISSIONER (INCOME TAX)

SCHOOLS

RELIGIOUS SERVICES

COMMUNITY ACTIVITIES

WEDDING RECEPTIONS

The mayor of Conwy Coun R E Roberts (as Constable of the Castle) with the golden key to the Castle. Coun Mrs V McDonald was the deputy mayor

Salute at Plas Mawr (l-r): Mrs A Bitowski, Coun Reg Roberts, the mayor; Wyn Roberts MP; and Mr M Pattinson (mayor's consort)

This shows the Constable's pennant in front of the mayor at the A.G.M., the pennant is later given to a representative of CADW to be flown on the castle

The mayor of Conwy (coun R E Roberts) with the plaque which was placed at Mount Pleasant by Conwy Town Council. This was to commemorate the cutting of the sod on St David's Day 1845 for the commencement of the railway at Conwy

The police escort for the mayor's procession in 1921

Castle Street with a parade on 25th August, 1909 to mark the motor car presented to Dr R A Pritchard, ex mayor of Conwy

The first three honorary burgesses of Conwy (councillors with 25 years service). Coun E M Pattinson, Bryn H Hughes and R J Thomas. The Marquis of Anglesey, made the presentation; since then G M Hackworth & R E Roberts have been made burgesses

Ex-constables of Conwy with the mayor Mrs J H Williams "year of the castles" 1983

Left: Councillor G M Hackworth toasting the new Mayor

Below: The Marquis of Anglesey, presenting plaques to the three new burgesses. The town clerk, Mrs Mary Battersby is on the right

Conwy Borough Council outside Bodlondeb 1970

A civic occasion at Bodlondeb with the Rev D Thomas (vicar) and mayor E D Rowlands

Conwy Castle. D Lloyd George receiving the Honorary Freedom of the Borough, 1923

Honorary Freedom of Conwy being presented to Dr M J Morgan JP., Mr Hugh Parry and Miss
Roberts (representing Mr Edward Roberts)

The past mayors of Aberconwy including the only Jackdaw in its brief history, the then mayor of 1987

Here E M Pattinson is being congratulated by her daughter, Fl. Lieut. B A Pattinson

Mayor's Parade, 1989 at the Vicarage Car Park

The mayor (Coun R W Springfield) unveils a plaque on behalf of Conwy Town Council to commemorate one of the best kept secrets of World War II; the building of sections of the Mulberry Harbour at Conwy, for use in the D Day invasion

Cutting the tape at Telford 150 on the old suspension bridge.
The tape was cut by the Marquis of Anglesey

You would be forgiven for thinking this was a civic event but the coach outside the Conway Castle Hotel is promoting local fish!

Mrs Gwenda Simpson, daughter of Dr M J Morgan presenting her father's Freedom Scroll to the mayor, E M Pattinson on behalf of Conwy Town Council

The Golden Key given to Dr Morgan on the opening of the Town Hall, 1st May, 1899

Above: General Booth
(Founder of the Salvation
Army) in Conwy Castle,
circa 1912

Left: A military parade at
the castle

Right: A scene
with the Royal
Engineers Church
Service, 1918

Above: Funeral of Wm. Allan, headmaster, 1911

Funeral of a soldier from Morfa Camp

Above: A military funeral 1909

Above: Dr Pritchard's funeral 1912

Dr Pritchard's
funeral 1912

Above and below: A funeral of a Crosville employee in the early part of the 20ᵗʰ century; it looks like Mr A Wood leading the mourners

Over leaf left/right: This funeral procession appears to be coming from Bodlondeb. Was it A Wood's funeral? *Bottom:* Four young Conwy ladies. Two of them lost fiances in the 1ˢᵗ World War – Susan Ellen and Sarah Roberts; they never married

Four views (this page and overleaf) of the Peace Day Celebrations, Castle Square, 19th July, 1919

Bangor Road with a parade led by Conwy Town Band

Royal British Legion passing St John's Methodist Church – Armistice Parade

Salute at Plas Mawr, Armistice Day, 1989, Mayor (Councillor Mrs K Smith)

V E Day Commemoration Service at Lancaster Square in 1995, 50 years on

Armistice Service at the cenotaph in Bodlandeb, 1990. Mayor R I Thomas B.E.M., Vicar Rev P R Jones with the representatives of Royal British Legion and Conwy Town Council

Conwy Castle. Peace Thanksgiving Service, 6th July, 1919

Taken in Castle Street, this records the visit of a French Admiral to Conwy. The mayor of Mametz also visited a number of North Wales towns including Conwy after the 1st World War

The British Red Cross

Standard Bearers of the Royal British Legion at Bodlondeb

An early infants class

Rosehill Street School, circa 1938

Boys' School, Rosehill Street

Girls' School, Bodlondeb

Girls School, Conwy

The Boys Brigade at Llandudno Junction

An infants class at Bodlondeb with Miss Parry (above) and with Mrs Jones, the Head Mistress (below)

Children Bodlondeb School

A class at Cadnant School

> "Manora",
> Cadnant Park;
> CONWAY.
> 6TH September, 1939.

I have been requested to send in reports of all cases where persons refused to accept evacuees presented at houses for admittance on Sunday and Monday last.

Will all Billeting Officers kindly make out each report on a separate sheet of paper, and let me have the same as soon as possible.

> (MRS) B. RALPHES.
> Secretary.

Facsimile of a letter concerning evacuee children of World War II

The Central School, April 1926

May Queen at Bodlondeb

Fancy Dress Day

Above: another view of the May Queen; Miss Myfanwy Jones is the headmistress

Right: Mrs B Roberts, the Headmistress, with one of her charges and an exhibition of class work

Two early views of the Girl's school

Social & Other Events

Welsh Day showing Conwy Church Mothers' Union with the children of Rev G J Roberts – Eiflyn & Olwen in Welsh costume

Vicarage grounds of Conwy Church with a very early Mothers' Union tea

PEACE ON EARTH
GOODWILL TOWARDS MEN.

Suffragettes. They spoke from carts on Conwy Quay. These were also shaken by the men who also heckled them. One card from Trefriw says "We are going to Conway to see the suffragettes perform"

The Mothers' Union in the vicarage grounds with the vicar Rev J W Roberts. On the left can be seen Gwladys Roberts, Sarah Roberts and Bob Jones helping

Is this the Darby & Joan? Some well known Conwy ladies may be recognised

Fire station. Town Ditch No 1 Platoon Conwy of 1st Caerns Home Guard. They won the challenge cup – bombing; bayonet fighting; rifle drill and Lewis gun team work

Welsh Day (1ˢᵗ March), showing the Conwy Womens' Institute

A 78th birthday party celebration in 1951 with Alderman and Mrs B V Hughes present

Above and below: St. Michael's Hall and its interior. Regular dances were held here during World War II

Snooker winners with some well known local gentlemen

Conwy Church Choir, 1920

Conwy Vicarage Grounds, with Ysgolion Eglwys Conwy (Conwy Church Sunday Schools)

1st Conwy Scouts 1914. W O Roberts was playing the Bugle. Most young men in the picture saw service in France, whilst still in their teens.

Patrol leader W O Roberts of the 1st Conwy Troop in 1913 or 1914

Brownies pass their saluting base, the ancient steps of Plas Mawr

The presentation of a print by the Round Table to Conwy's Voluntary Elderly Centre (Clwb yr Efail), at the Smithy Centre . This centre won the Prince of Wales award

The Conwy church trip from Lancaster Square with everybody in their Sunday best for the outing

The Royal Engineers marching through Lancaster Square on their way to the church

Royal British Legion Jubilee Dinner, 1935

Conwy Royal British Legion – Womens' Section give Christmas Dinner to Pensioners; Father Christmas and helpers are thanked for their work

Conwy Civic Society Dinner at The Castle Hotel. (l-r): Mrs Shaw; Mr Shaw; Mrs R H Pritchard; Mr R H Pritchard; Mrs E M Pattinson; Ednyfed Hudson Davies MP; Mrs Wyn Roberts; Michael Senior; M Pattinson

Aberconwy Historical Society Dinner at The Castle Hotel. G Griffiths; Mrs Griffiths; Mrs M Springfield, Mayoress and Mr R W Springfield, mayor; John Hughes, Chief executive of Aberconwy

Left: Conwy Special Constables' Annual Dinner, March 1943

Below: The Sergeants Mess St David's Dinner, 25th March, 1939. It was held in the Drill Hall, Berry Street which has now been demolished

Royal British Legion Womens' Section Christmas Dinner. Mrs E Carr, Mrs Jones, Mrs A Gregory, Mrs Hughes, Mrs M Ball, Mrs C Jones, Mrs J D Porter, Mrs W Marshall, Mrs E M Pattinson, Mrs N Craven, Mrs A Robertson, Mrs J Robertson

Lady Mostyn presenting a statue to Mrs E M Pattinson for services to The Royal National Lifeboat Institution

Konwy Karnival Knights in Lancaster Square. W Llewelyn Hughes was the mascot

Another view of visitors at the castle prior to the loss of the arch and before the removal of the trees flanking the castle itself

Castle Square in 1920/30 showing motor cars of important visitors

A later scene at the same spot, with long queues to go through the toll gate. The toll money went to
Conwy Bridge Commissioners who spent it on improvements and the old borough celebrations

Three views of early motor
cars in Conwy

The vicar's car with the vicar, J W Roberts and R Jones, his chauffeur

These visitors had to rely on this elegant coach

Silver Motor Bus parked near the castle

Another queue at the tollgate. Note that the trees have now gone

Kelly of Conwy, Guardian to Conway Bridge. The famous goose adopted the town, and the town adopted him. He was well known the world over, and thousands came to see "Kelly". He died in 1925

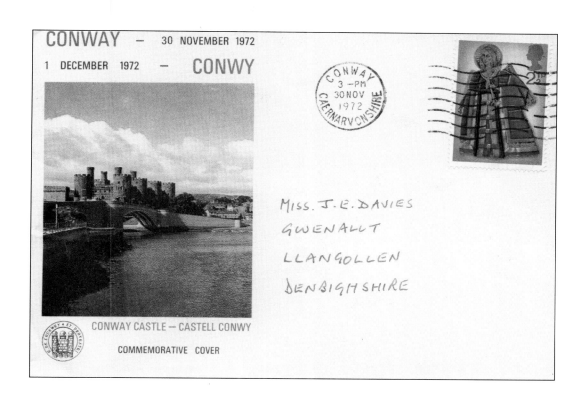

Changing the name of Conway, 30th November, 1972 …. to Conwy, 1st December 1972

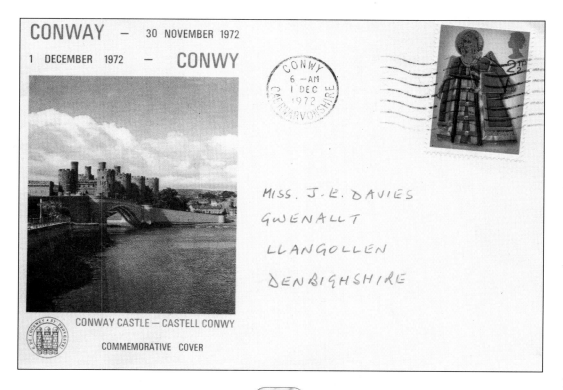

LANDMARK COLLECTOR'S LIBRARY

Mining Histories

- Collieries of South Wales: Vol 1   *ISBN: 1 84306 015 9, £22.50*
- Collieries of South Wales: Vol 2   *ISBN: 1 84306 017 5, £19.95*
- Collieries of Somerset & Bristol   *ISBN: 1 84306 029 9, £14.95*
- Copper & Lead Mines around the Manifold Valley, North Staffordshire   *ISBN: 1 901522 77 6, £19.95*
- Images of Cornish Tin   *ISBN: 1 84306 020 5, £29.95*
- Lathkill Dale, Derbyshire, its Mines and Miners   *ISBN: 1 901522 80 6, £8.00*
- Rocks & Scenery the Peak District   *ISBN: 1 84306 026 4, paperback, £7.95*
- Swaledale, its Mines & Smelt Mills   *ISBN: 1 84306 018 3, £19.95*

Industrial Histories

- Alldays and Onions   *ISBN: 1 84306 047 7, £24.95*
- The Life & Inventions of Richard Roberts, 1789 -1864   *ISBN: 1 84306 027 2, £29.95*
- The Textile Mill Engine   *ISBN: 1 901522 43 1, paperback, £22.50*
- Watt, James, His Life in Scotland, 1736-74   *ISBN 1 84306 045 0, £29.95*
- Wolseley, The Real, Adderley Park Works, 1901-1926   *ISBN 1 84306 052 3, £19.95*
- Morris Commercial   *ISBN: 1 84306 069 8 (Price to be announced)*

Roads & Transportantion

- Packmen, Carriers & Packhorse Roads   *ISBN: 1 84306 016 7, £19.95*
- Roads & Trackways of Wales   *ISBN: 1 84306 019 1, £22.50*
- Welsh Cattle Drovers   *ISBN: 1 84306 021 3, £22.50*
- Peakland Roads & Trackways   *ISBN: 1 901522 91 1, £19.95*

Regional/Local Histories

- Colwyn Bay, Its History across the Years   *ISBN: 1 84306 014 0, £24.95*
- Crosses of the Peak District   *ISBN 1 84306 044 2, £14.95*
- Derbyshire Country Houses: Vol 1   *ISBN: 1 84306 007 8, £19.95*
- Derbyshire Country Houses: Vol 2   *ISBN: 1 84306 041 8, £19.95*
- Historic Hallamshire   *ISBN: 1 84306 049 3, £19.95*
- Llandudno: Queen of Welsh Resorts   *ISBN 1 84306 048 5, £15.95*
- Llanrwst: the History of a Market Town   *ISBN 1 84306 070 1, £14.95*
- Lost Houses in and around Wrexham   *ISBN 1 84306 057 4, £16.95*
- Lost Houses of Derbyshire   *ISBN 1 84306 064 7, £19.95, October 02*
- Shipwrecks of North Wales   *ISBN: 1 84306 005 1, £19.95*
- Shrovetide Football and the Ashbourne Game   *ISBN: 1 84306 063 9, £19.95*
- Well Dressing   *ISBN: 1 84306 042 6, Full colour, £19.95*

Full details upon request

LANDMARK
Publishing Ltd ● ■ ●

Ashbourne Hall, Cokayne Ave, Ashbourne, Derbyshire, DE6 1EJ England
Tel 01335 347349 Fax 01335 347303
e-mail landmark@clara.net web site: www.landmarkpublishing.co.uk

Index

A
Aberconwy Historical Society 180
Aberconwy House 77, 79, 104
Albion Vaults 89
Armistice Day 156
Armistice Parade 155
Automobile Palace 60

B
Baptist Chapel 120
Bazaar 89
Berry Street 70, 71, 72, 84, 103, 181
Black Lion 81
Blue Bell 78
British Legion 86, 155, 157, 159, 179, 182
Bron Castell 103
Brownies 177
Bull's Head 67, 105
Burgesses 134, 135, 139

C
Cadnant School 91, 165
Caerns Home Guard 171
Castle Square 184
Castle Street 47, 70-84, 103, 120, 134, 138, 158
Cenotaph 97, 99, 126, 133, 157
Central School 91
Church Choir 174
Church Street 85, 86
Cinema 67, 81
Civic Sunday 132, 133
Coach & Horses Inn 105
Coffee Tavern 79
College, The 27, 83, 87
Conway Arms 77
Conwy Castle 17-34, 35, 37, 84, 106, 109, 118
Conwy Fair 70, 82
Conwy Special Constables' 181
Conwy Town Band 155
Cross, The 72
Crown Tavern 67

D
Darby & Joan 171
Drill Hall 181
Duke and Duchess of York 106

E
Eagles Buildings 74
Eagles Inn 74
Erskine Family & Commercial Hotel 85

F
Fire station 21, 22, 171
Fireman 129

G
General Booth 147
George, Lloyd 113, 127, 128, 142
Grosvenor Café 60
Guildhall 20, 75, 132, 134, 135

H
H.M. The Queen 44, 111, 112
H.R.H. Princess Margaret 109, 110
High Street 62-69, 72, 103, 105

J
Jackdaw 65, 99, 122, 143

K
Konwy Karnival Knights 183

L
Lancaster Square 50-61, 120, 156, 178, 183
Liverpool Arms 94

M
Mail Coach Inn 105
Marquis of Anglesey 139, 140, 145
Mothers' Union 169, 170
Mulberry Harbour 144

O
Oakwood Park Hotel 97

P
Park Hall 100
Parlwr Mawr 99
Parry Watch 43, 65
Peace Day 153
Peace Thanksgiving Service 158
Plas Isa Place 69
Plas Mawr 62, 63, 64, 66, 67, 104, 133, 136

Plas Mawr Restaurant 68
Plough seat 120
Police 131, 138, 135
Post Office 59, 61
Prince of Wales 16, 62, 109, 177

R
Red Cross 159
R'odyn, The 92-96, 113
Rosehill Street 85, 86, 129, 131, 134, 160
Rosemary Lane 87
Royal Engineers 57, 147, 178
Royal Oak Tavern 92
Royal Welch Fusiliers 111

S
Scouts 116, 120, 130, 175, 176
Smallest House 26, 92, 95, 113
Smithy 87, 177
St Agnes Road 87
Stryd y Burum 84
Sunday Schools 175
Suspension Bridge 21, 22, 38, 134, 145
Swan, The 71

T
Telford Thomas 122, 123, 124, 134, 145
Thatcher, Margaret 115
Town Hall 81, 134, 135, 146

U
Uppergate Street 87, 88, 89

V
V E Day Commemoration Service 156
Voluntary Elderly Centre 177

W
Woodlands, The 100

Y
Y Groes 72